Fireborn

By: Sarah Shelton

Thank you for picking up a book written by a small writer. This is my first book (it is completely unedited, so I'm so sorry for any mistakes).

Writing poetry was something I was never naturally good at. I wrote throughout high school, knowing nothing about poetry. In undergraduate college, I took a poetry class which inspired me to just write from the heart with free/blank verse poetry (and some other types, such as haikus and sonnets—which I labeled so you can see what I was going for). So far I have learned that the more you read and write poetry, the better you get.

I am not very creative, but I love expressing my feelings and am beginning to appreciate the words that come from my head.

I hope you enjoy the journey as you read, and hopefully, my writing will improve even more in my next book!

I'd also like to give Selena Gomez a special thanks for inspiring me for so many years, as well as Taylor Swift for inspiring me to not be afraid to publish my vulnerable words.

Without further ado, here are some of my (updated) high school, college, and graduate school excerpts.

Fireborn

Fire in my lungs,

since I was young—

born under a Leo moon.

Pride and ego,

passion and energy,

flowing through my veins

A warm embrace

or raging beast,

fire is a relentless enemy.

A glowing friend,

Or hungry predator,

located in the deepest part of myself.

Rainy Nights

a night of loneliness,
raindrops pelting,
glistening on the window,

a host of street lights play as candles
in the dark apartment.
a romantic abode, one for herself.

eyes half open,
lights begin to glimmer,
reaching out to her.

The rain quiets down,
singing a soft lullaby,
ready to dream of a land far away.

Beachy

Sticky juice soaks down my arm,
biting a freshly picked peach.
Wind flows through my chestnut hair,
my arm held high, blocking the sun
from burning my hazel eyes.

The waves crash at my feet,
salt water soaking into my calluses.
A flock of seagulls fly around my head,
wondering when I'll share
my succulent treat.

Pacing along the beach,
the scorching sand tickles my heels,
and the washed-up shells pinch my toes.
Now I know,
this is where I belong.

I head to the car,
My feet melting on the pavement,

ready to face

the ice-cold truth,

It's not ready for me yet.

I continue my journey home,

to the small apartment,

far from the ocean,

far from the fresh berries,

far from the brine air.

Shipwreck - Haiku

Lye ashore, beach breeze—
now one with the ocean sand.
Nightfall, here I stay.

Golden Brown

My first love ended horribly,
when all I needed was clarity.

Young and in love,
stupid and gullible.

Listening to the whispers of others;
from friends, strangers, and future lovers.

I was tricked and fooled
leaving an internal wound.

As I looked into those golden-brown eyes,
one last time, I knew everything was a lie.

Goodbye.

Untitled (Sonnet)

Emotions on a whim, coasters of love.
Heart filled to the brim with the love I bleed.
For you, I will go beyond and above,
holding onto you, hunger full of greed.

Carousel horses, running from the spins.
Stomach butterflies fluttering away.
Watching this crazy love as it begins,
like a senior high school fairytale play.

Jealousy fills the room with sinful air,
generational bliss, it's not your fault.
Nervous love is something I cannot bear.
I ran, bringing love to a screeching halt.

Sometimes, a certain person is not right;
Loving wrong will always come back to bite.

Tangled in the Branches

I want to be free,

like a kite in the wind.

But as I lay my head on the satin pillow,

the flashbacks haunt me;

like a ghost trying to taunt me.

I blink three times and whisper,

"Go away."

The kite is stuck in a tree.

Why can't it just let me be free?

Sunset - Haiku

Cherry blossom skies,
swirls of beaming bright sunlight,
slowly fade to dark.

Fired

She was a fire,
A burning light.
A source of energy,
A campfire night.

He was water,
A damp cloud.
A dirty swamp,
Melting snow, ready to be plowed.

He covered her light,
melting in the rain.
She didn't know the cause,
He was to blame.

Obsessed (sonnet)

Followed in the halls, a dark alleyway.
Wherever I go, your presence follows.
Please loosen your grip, I am not your prey.
You always pull me back with your wallows.

I yearn for freedom, but you won't allow.
To you, I am an object, only yours.
I am sure you already planned your vow,
All you do is create my life detour.

But you have been warned, I'm not in love
You threatened yourself, but I'm not your dove.

Name

Your name used to bring sorrow and ache,
but now with ice in my veins,
and a heart full of novocaine,
it doesn't quite feel the same.

Prom

Happiness in her eyes,

As she looked in a mirror,

the first time she was awed

at her own reflection.

A blue navy dress, fitting just right.

Blonde curls and silver sparkles across her eyes.

A corsage around her wrist, black and white stripes,

to match her black and glitter nails.

A smile stayed across her lips,

even though it wasn't her scene.

That one look in the mirror, her anxiety faded.

A real-life princess for one night,

Just like she always dreamed.

Gardens - Haiku

Universe of life,
Mother Nature, please bless me
with beauty and grace.

i want my youth back

loved and used,

tricked and abused.

now confused

as to why I stayed.

stole my body

and youth,

then refused

to acknowledge my truth.

pushed me until i shattered,

framed me in the wreckage,

to paint everyone a lousy picture,

of who you made me out to be.

you spun my world,

left me grasping at pieces,

all because you were bored.

i want my youth back, the best version of me.

New

New freckles formed,
from the summer sun's kisses
reminding me there are parts of me,
that he hasn't seen or touched.

My hair now reaches my back,
blonde roots peeking out from my scalp,
reminding me that I change faster
than a Manhattan train.

My old sneakers, dirty and grim
reminding me I need a new pair,
ones that didn't travel the country,
with sorrow in the back of my mind.

We all grow into something new.
Change is inevitable.
Embrace and acceptance
is the key to something new.

Capricorn - Haiku

The sun shone as I
entered Earth. Ruled by Saturn,
ambitious, I am.

Dance

She danced like a baby swan,
landing in water.
Beauty and brawn,
she was a solo act.

Music on blast in a lone room,
She roams from each side,
a jump with each boom.
Arms swaying like a playground swing.

Toes tapping on the floor,
while the iridescent lights shine above.
A night with her was never a bore,
a night alone, with her music and twirls.

Marley

He placed his chin
into my cupped hand,
Like he knew it was time.
He waited for me to come back,
to say thank you and goodbye.

He wanted me by his side.
He was full of love.
Innocence still sparkled in his eyes,
Just like the day he came home,
twelve years before.

Perhaps we should all be
as loving as animals.
Exploring the planet with glee,
and kissing the faces of those we love,
while tears fall down their cheeks.

Saying goodbye is the hardest part,
But we will never truly be a part.

Signs

My Angel, watch me from the clouds,
As I look for you in crowds.

My Angel, how I miss you dearly.
Without you, life hasn't been as cheery.

My Angel, every little white dog is a sign,
a sign you're still here, a sign you're still mine.

My Angel, you left a scar on my heart,
but one day we will no longer be apart.

April

An April return,
Crocus buds peak through the dirt.
The bumble bees swarm the flower beds
with joy. The pounding rain
quenches the flower's thirst.
The sun peeks through the clouds,
providing the heat
that has been missing for months.
The birds chirp, alerting their friends
of the breakfast bread,
thrown out the window
by their neighbor's mother.
Out of hibernation, returning for warmth
The animals coo at the long return of April.

Heartbreak on the Lake

Disappointment rang through the air,

like rotten candy bars on a campfire night.

Heartbreaks and cabins full of tears.

Rain patters, turning the soil to mush.

His story is a canoe full of holes

and as cheap as a tent full of ants and mold.

The trees sway in the wind, sharing our secrets—

of the girl who was lied to,

and the boy who just went home.

Betrayal (sonnet)

Feeling of betrayal falls from my eyes
in the form of tears. Temporarily
stained into my cheeks. The multi-year lie
hits like a punch, leaving my trust weary.

Pain cuts off my voice, so I cannot speak.
My body starts to feel numb, like my heart.
Try to pull myself up, but I'm too weak,
Getting out of bed is the hardest part.

I was truly fooled. I feel so useless.
Lies are triggering, forever, always.
All that you did to me is excuseless.
I don't even know why I care these days.

It's not about you or me. It's blatant
lies. An internal wound, one that's latent.

Burned

Before she was fire,
she was nature,
calming evergreens,
a home for all beings.

She provided and gave,
rose gardens and soothing rivers,
until she was burned,
from heartbreak and fear.

The sadness took over,
a forest fire ensued.
She arose from the ashes,
contemplating her next move.

Happy Place
(An Autobiographical Letter)

Someone asked me,
"What is your happy place?"
I said my bed.
We laughed.

But then I remember the nights,
The long solo fights.
while I snuggled into my twin-sized bed,
A Pandora's Box ready to be opened.

A night of calm, then out of the blue—
You crashed, always reminding me,
I'm not good enough,
I'm not her, and I'm not you.

Built up stress,
a thunderstorm brewing,
only when we were alone, in the dark,
when nobody else could hear.

Shivering like a sad puppy,
caught in the rain—
Waiting for you to throw something,
as Godzilla always did best.

Your words cut like a broken window,
glass shards blowing around the room.
Your voice shattered my heart,
It felt like bear claws tearing me apart.

I never fought back,
as the fear of your permanent leave
crushed me. But then I'd catch your smile, as you
watched me wipe my snot and tears on my sleeve.

Leaving the ghost of your words
echoing through four tiny walls.
I needed to empty my feelings,
my body sensing danger, deep within my belly.

My bed became a scary place.
Running my hands on the ash-gray comforter

no longer brought ease.

It was tainted. No longer my home base.

But I guess I'm healed now,

Because now that you have been gone,

my bed is once again

a happy place.

- Sar

Autoimmune

Aches, pains,
nausea, and migraines
keep me up at night.

methotrexate and SSRIs,
a big medication supply,
I seem to have.

Many appointments and bloodwork
but not sick enough for perks,
working until I cannot stand.

Health bills are lining up,
feels like a pileup,
with little to no answers.

I just seem to scream and yelp,
and nobody knows how to help,
not even the doctors.

Graduation (Sonnet)

The chapter left me shaken to the core.
The journey was a volcano bound to
erupt. Supposed to be ready to soar,
but I was too sick, and the pressure grew.

Ending in an unexpected earthquake,
life as I had known fell apart, crumbling.
Senior year, I was stuck in a dark place.
ended in a roar, it all went tumbling.

My hard work shattered, and I lost my spark.
I did not know how to continue on.
Lost friends, continued searching in the dark.
This entire journey just felt like a con.

I look back at my time now, healed and bright,
ready to continue using my light.

My Safe Place

I thought I'd never find a safe place,
after everything I went through,
But you became my base.

I learned I'm unlovable,
That I'll always be a disgrace,
but it's just not the case.

Now I have someone to embrace,
when I'm having a good day,
Or even during a bad headspace.

After being displaced,
for so long,
I now have a place.

New Haven Hike

We stand together
on top of West Rock,
hand in hand,
peaking over the edge.

The wispy clouds spread over the summer sky,
The heat devours us, my throat begging for a drink.
We sit on the coffee-brown stone,
enjoying an iced tea, with the occasional kiss.

We soak in the sun,
looking over the university skyline,
taking pictures and sharing stories
with trees swaying behind us.

Once darkness fills the sky, it's time to climb down.
The rain begins to hit the leaves above us,
laughter filling the air,
ready to make our way back home.

Summer Love

Looking at you is a summer's day,
a golden retriever fetching a frisbee,
sun rays shooting at our eyes
in a field of tulips,
laughter filling the park.

Winds may shake the trees,
while cold rain hits,
bringing me shivers
But you quickly grab the umbrella,
from your car's passenger door.

Summer lasts forever with you,
The sun shall not fade,
Clouds come and go,
But love remains strong,
always.

Puddles - Haiku

Jumping in puddles,
like a child stuck in the rain.
Healing inner me.

Spring Day (sonnet)

Colorful swirls of clouds fill the sky, like

a cumulus marshmallow with pink cream.

Some get ready to bike or take a hike.

Perfect day, a stroll of delight and dreams.

Birds chirping, seeking a fresh morning bath;

Squirrels sneakily chomping on bird seed,

leaving crumbs for those to follow the path.

Geese flocking in the yard, just what they need.

Flowers peek out the mulch, hungry for rain,

while bumble bees sip on their sweet nectar.

Kids run home from school, knees full of grass stains,

animals hide from lads in their sector.

Spring is a season to share the outdoors,

but, don't forget to get enough night snores.

Texas Snow Cone- Haiku

Coconut snow cones,
melting under sunny skies,
A Grand Prairie Trip.

Flight Home (Draft)

Awaiting the journey home

A bustling airport,

nodding out from the holiday.

A buzzing intercom,

trudging away to the gate.

Throwing suitcases into the compartment,

Coughs, yawns, and cries filling the cabin.

Jumping into the window seat,

buckled up, cuddled with a jacket,

ready for a stiff-necked nap.

Awakening for descending,

How did we get here?

Turning heads face the window,

houses sparkling like Christmas lights,

up above in the dark New York sky.

Rainbows Save Lives - Pride (villanelle)

It's a great day for glitter and rainbows.
The fast train whips by, my red hair flies back;
I am ready to sit by the window.

Gems, flags, flower crowns, and glitter eyeshadow.
We all cram into the cart on the track
Excitement fills all, flags wave of rainbows.

red, green, orange, blue, purple, and yellow.
We reach the city with a halting smack,
Grand Central is right through the window.

Rainbow flags, sandwiches with no mayo,
We stand on the sidelines as a pack.
cheering, dancing, and signs full of rainbows.

Plenty of life-saving resources and photos,
We start to leave as the sky shifts black.
Time went by fast, like looking out of a window.

On our way back to the average life flow
Time to wipe off the red and lilac
eyeshadow. Goodbye to the other rainbows.
Now I am back to looking out the window.

Acceptance

Cold in my heart,

as a wintery silence.

The top of a mountain,

shivering from an arctic breeze.

Broken and hurt,

like an abandoned stray.

Crying in the rain,

A melting iceberg,

crashing down,

a tower of cards,

in the flowing wind

of acceptance and love.

Tattoo

The scripture on my arm

reminds me to love myself first.

Inked forever, seeped into my skin.

A constant reminder of the past,

when I needed the advice the most.

The empathy that's supposed

to be a greater good, left sorrow

stained into my heart. Now, a deep black line

in my inner elbow. A cursive body of work,

a visible blemish of my past.

"Love Yourself First"

Thorns (Draft)

A thorn bush in a world full of roses.

She wants to be loved,

but others judge her exterior.

If not handled right,

she can be a prickly bite.

A cuddly porcupine,

still navigating their way.

Still a danger,

no matter how tame,

or how sweet,

she can be.

A resting state of anger,

But is it you?

Or is it me?

Winter Snow

Powdered sugar falling from heaven,
like a spilled fried dough at a county fair.
Wind whispers secrets through the barren trees,
While icicles hang from the alleyways.

The grass and branches are all dressed in white,
ready for their season-long celebration.
The birds and bears hide away in their nests, while
children run in the rhythm of the snowflakes' dance.

Sleds fly down the hills, falling in the spots
where squirrels buried their snacks not long ago.
Plows run down the road,
throwing snow wherever it may go.

Snowmen are brought back to life, once again
some with their top hats and carrot noses,
ready to one day melt from the luminous light,
their life path that they must follow.

Winter Steps

The brisk air whips against my face as the last leaves from autumn fall crackle under my feet. Cloudy sky dims above us as my dog's tan-wirehaired ears flop with each step.

The clanking metal of his two "Milo" name tags dies down every time he steps off the sidewalk to stop at each plant to sniff, clearly missing the summer greens.

I peek at the faded red brick walls of the elementary school, as Milo smells the nearby bushes. Memories from past recess days fill my mind as we loop around the empty campus, step off the property, and walk toward the edge of the dusky road, ready to make our way home.

I press the frigid button on the metal machine in front of the faintly white-lined crosswalk, waiting for the walk symbol to blink. The cars on the road come to a screeching halt as the light turns red.

"Click Click Click." I quickly pull my dog by his lavender leash as we sprint across the indicated white lines. His toes tip-tap on the charcoal ground, nails scratching the dusty sidewalk, as he leaps up. The cars begin to rev up as the light flashes green.

We turn down the adjacent road, with winds shaking the dull-empty trees, as Milo sprints to the house he knows all too well, already preparing to cozy up under his rouge-red paw print blanket.

Modernization (sonnet)

The kitchen backsplash is now torn apart.
Azure blue tiles, now replaced with tan paint,
at least the child refrigerator art,
remains. As a kid, I made a complaint.

I love that blue wall, I cannot let go.
A hidden tile lay upon the dollhouse
roof. I love this kitchen; it always glows.
Dad knew, listen to the wishes of his spouse.

It was their kitchen after all, not mine.
I watched the white design torn from the floor,
now lies hardwood replica, which looks fine.
My childhood changing so fast left me sore.

Is it really about my child home,
or is it growing up? Missing my dome.

You're Art

You're broken heart,
Turned words into art.
YOUng bRokE heART

Pieces of me

A piece of me lies within
those who have entered my space,
Despite hatred in their veins.
admired and misunderstood.

My Future

A ring for the future,
bright and full of desire.
A crystallized diamond,
enthralled to put on my finger.

An embroidered tablecloth,
Fine china with golden swirls,
and mini spoons.
A dinner for two.

Moonlit nights,
dancing in the rain,
kissing under refrigerator lights,
bowls full of treats.

A cake full of pink cream,
bibs and cribs,
shelves full of memories
A manifestation I'm guiding.

Saying Goodbye to the Past

When the fire in you stops burning,

you will see the destruction you have created.

The mind can never be replaced,

But it can be rebuilt into something new.

Set my past ablaze, fireborn.

Dedicated to my Mom (Sonnet)

My truest best friend in life is my mom,
and I will never be ashamed of that.
She keeps me fed, she always keeps me calm,
and is always there when I need her, stat!

From attending my lame school chorus show,
to taking me to doctors at twenty,
to filling the tree with presents. I know,
My mom will forever love me plenty.

Couldn't have asked for a better mother.
She was put in my life for a reason.
We always mean the world to each other,
through every problem and every season.

Would like to thank you for being the best,
the part of where I have been so blessed.

Thank you for reading!

Sometimes it is hard to write, with brain fog
and dissociation issues. So I
will now write this. As if it were a blog.
Even if this sonnet is a bit dry.

Writer's block, creativity is slim.
I'm just trying to keep it together.
Living life and writing this on a whim,
this is coldly grim, like the night weather.

Not sure why I am at this computer,
when all I want to do is ugly cry.
I can't even think. I need a tutor.
It's near the end, I guess this is goodbye.

I cannot compete with other poets,
but this is me. I don't have an end rhyme.

www.ingramcontent.com/pod-product-compliance
Lightning Source LLC
Chambersburg PA
CBHW070634050426
42450CB00011B/3198